JAMES FAIRWEATHER

Britain's Youngest Serial Killer

by

C.L. Swinney

JAMES FAIRWEATHER

Britain's Youngest Serial Killer

by

C.L. Swinney

Copyrighted

RJ Parker Publishing, Inc.

06.2016

ISBN-13: 978-1533683991

ISBN-10: 1533683999

http://RJParkerPublishing.com/

Published in the United States of America

Copyrights

While the Publisher is responsible for the sales, marketing and distribution of a book, it is the author's obligation to ensure the accuracy of facts.

Table of Contents

Thank you to my Publisher, editor, proof-readers, and cover artist for your support:

- - **Chris**

RJ Parker Publishing, Aeternum Designs (book cover), Bettye McKee (editor), and

Proof-readers:

Lorrie Suzanne Phillippe, Marlene Fabregas, Darlene Horn, Ron Steed, Katherine McCarthy, Robyn MacEachern, Lee Knieper Husemann, Kathi Garcia, Vicky Matson-Carruth, & Linda H. Bergeron

----

“This is a work of nonfiction. No names have been changed, no characters invented, no events fabricated.”

– RJ Parker, PhD

Quotes

"So I started stabbing. One shot missed and went into his eye and I went into a rage. There was a big pool of blood."

- James Fairweather, 15, describing his first murder.

"I went behind her and the voices started laughing, I remember again they were really, really loud."

- Fairweather, 15, describing his second murder.

"As time went by they got louder, more aggressive, saying violent things. I felt they were my friends and I distanced myself from other people. People called me a 'freak' and a 'weirdo' because I was talking to myself."

- James describing his teenage years between the ages of 13 and 15 years old.

"James Fairweather is a monster in our eyes - and we will never be able to forgive him."

- Julie Finch, James Attfield's mother speaking about her son's killer.

"This boy would've been fantasizing about being a killer for some time before making the step from fantasy to reality and sometimes fantasies are made more real to a killer by research done online."

- PROFESSOR OF CRIMINOLOGY, DAVID WILSON, speaking about James Fairweather.

Prologue

Colchester, Essex, Britain

Believed to be the oldest known recorded town in Britain, Colchester began to take shape as far back as AD 79. At that time, Gaius Plinius Secundus, aka "Pliny the Elder," a Roman author as well as naval and army commander of the early Roman Empire, made mention of *Camulodunon* (Colchester) to his personal friend, Emperor Vespasian. That Colchester was among the discussions of educated and powerful men, clearly suggests how important the area was to the Romans and those who would eventually pass through. Interestingly enough, fellow beer enthusiasts will recognize "Pliny the Elder," since his unique name is used to pay homage to one of America's best Double India Pale Ales.

The quaint yet growing town never looked back after achieving lofty recognition in 79 A.D. Significant events, some on a regional and growing global scale, would help define the entire region for hundreds of years. The Stour Valley Riots of 1642 and the Colchester earthquake in 1884, two such events, shaped the culture and attitude of its residents. One could spend weeks attempting to discern the true identity of Colchester, what makes the community tick nowadays, but that is not the focus of this book.

Sadly, a recent tragedy has placed Colchester on center stage, even on an international scale, after one of its teenaged residents, a fifteen-year-old boy named James Fairweather, was recently found guilty of two horrific murders. Making matters even worse, the child, now seventeen years old, has been labeled as Britain's youngest serial killer. It's not often the words 'child' and 'serial killer' are used in the same sentence or conversation.

Although James Fairweather maliciously and deliberately killed two innocent people, this case could actually have been far worse. By his own admission, Fairweather confessed that he was planning to kill at least fifteen more people had he not been apprehended by law enforcement. Wrap your mind around that for a moment.

The number has never set well with me since researching this case.

I cannot even fathom that a child could harbor such thoughts, and to be honest, it scares the hell out of me. If his acts and his thoughts are any indication of where things are headed with our young people in our cultures, we have a serious problem on our hands. Pay attention and digest the meaning of this case and this book. Form your own thoughts, but I warn you now, much of what we are going to discuss will hit you square in the mouth. Some of you may even look at your own children, compare them to what Fairweather was doing prior to his first killing, and have an epiphany.

The danger factors indicating that James Fairweather was a "loose cannon" were plainly obvious. The signs he exhibited on a daily basis pointed to him being a disturbed child in a complete tailspin. Yet no one did anything to pull him out of his mental downward spiral.

One might argue that when he killed the first time, it was too late in that stage of his life to intervene and likely save human life, but I disagree. His behavior could have been curtailed before ever killing someone. The judicial system in the United Kingdom dropped the ball with young James Fairweather. In doing so, two wonderful and greatly loved and admired individuals were senselessly murdered...by a teenager.

By no means will I try to explain away or rationalize the behavior and actions of James Fairweather. However, the fact remains that it's my opinion the murders he committed could have been prevented, or if nothing else, a second murder by his hands should never have happened. In fact, were it not for a nosy hairdresser out walking her dog, Fairweather would have remained on a killing spree until he slipped up, a witness came forward, or police caught him. In a creepy sidebar note, the same hairdresser who cracked this serial killer case wide open, according to Fairweather, was his next target.

Once you've read this book, I think you'll feel the same unnerving feelings I had while I researched this case. As I digested the things that contributed to turning a child into a sadistic serial killer, I was reminded of recent events across the United States and abroad having similar undertones. Young killers seem to be on the rise and we read about their cases far too often. We must as a civilization reconsider what our young people are doing with their time and make every effort to steer them in a better direction. By no means am I saying we should lock our kids away and live in fear, but there's something to be said about playing hide-and-go-seek and *talking* instead of texting with friends. Right now, our children are mesmerized and "hooked" by video games, they are slaves to social media, and they are targeted daily by billion dollar corporations far more interested in the almighty dollar than what the future holds.

The James Fairweather case completely supports the reason why I'm a true crime writer and why I've focused so much of my attention lately on serial killers. If any of my readers see someone, a child or adult, who acts as James Fairweather did for years prior to his first kill, please alert law enforcement. I've been in law enforcement for almost seventeen years. I'm telling you from the perspective of a deputy sheriff that you need to make the call or flag down an officer and tell them about people like James Fairweather.

Programs, systems, counseling, and a host of other services exist to help these folks, but none of them work if the people who need them aren't exposed to them or at least turned in the right direction. They won't get introduced to the services on their own because they see nothing wrong with their thoughts and actions. Not all of these types of people can be saved, but even saving a few of them and curtailing the sick plans they've dreamed about for years would be worth the effort.

Consider that you, a soul among billions of others, could actually save the lives of potential victims and possibly the lives of probable serial killers by simply getting involved. Stay on the periphery if you'd like, but don't turn your back completely. Law enforcement around the planet relies on the input of the people they serve. Although some of you may argue, we have only one set of eyes and they don't always see everything.

Chapter One: The Murder of James Attfield

Colchester, Essex, March 29, 2014

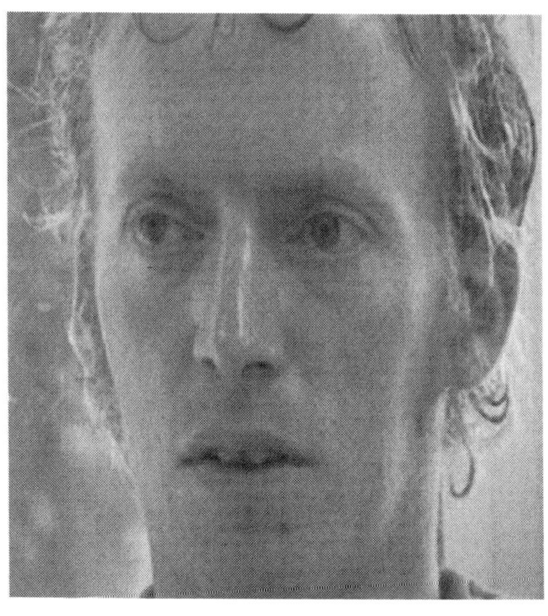

James Attfield, murdered by 15-year-old serial killer James Fairweather.

James Attfield, a father of five lovely children, passed through Castle Park just after midnight looking for a place to have some beers. He stumbled upon the River Lodge Pub, located at 20-22 Middleborough overlooking the River Colne; for several hours he drank with friends and a few bar patrons. James spent quite a bit of time hanging out in the pub and perhaps had a bit too much to drink. Realizing he'd had enough, he used the restroom, said his "Goodbyes," and wandered along Riverside Walk until finding a spot to sit down and gather his thoughts.

Not only was the alcohol playing havoc on his decision-making ability, but he still suffered from the lingering effects of brain damage he suffered as a result of an automobile accident in 2010. Obviously we can't know for sure what led James to be where he was, why he chose the location he did to stop, but it does not matter. At some point, he fell asleep in the grass just a few paces from River Colne. It appears he slept in the location for over an hour before being spotted by a child looking for his first victim.

Unbeknownst to James was the fact that a fifteen-year-old boy, whose mind was completely lost and cluttered with various alleged psychotic voices ordering him to kill someone, lurked in the shadows along Riverside Walk. There was a strong sense of urgency in these voices within the youngster's head. They spoke of him needing to make a sacrifice. If he did not, the voices would come and kill him instead. These were the voices that fueled the killer and directed him to do things most people would find unbelievable. But to him, the conversations, which supposedly began when he was twelve years old, were completely normal. They brought him to a safe place and were the only ones who understood him.

This child, later identified as serial killer James Fairweather, stroked a folding knife in his jacket pocket as visions of violent killings he'd seen in video games flashed before him. He cracked a wry smile and realized he was eager to hunt and kill a human. He'd walked along city streets and found no one based on the hour, so he worked his way toward River Colne. James had a thing for trails and the water, but only the voices in his head knew that. He began to get frustrated when he could not find another person out and about. Despite the chaos in his head, one particular voice, among the most angry and violent he ever spoke to, continually chanted, "Kill. Kill. Kill."

Truly there was no way to tell who his victim would be, but he was sure he would murder someone, anyone, before the night was over.

Then, whether it was chance or fate, James Fairweather spotted a man lying in some grass and the same demented and extremely powerful voice from earlier told him, "He's the one, do it." James reached into his jacket, grabbed his knife, and unfolded the blade. He could see that the person was a man and it appeared he was asleep, or maybe drunk and passed out. Fairweather later recalled that when he saw James Attfield sleeping, he assumed the man was drunk and that he could kill him easily because he would have no idea of the pending attack until it was too late. He also stated that at that very moment, when he knew he was about to kill a man, he was extremely excited -- more excited than he could ever recall.

It must be mentioned that at that very moment, Fairweather should never have been out on the streets in the first place. Just three days prior, he'd been convicted of using a knife to hold up a shop while he stole items. He wore his school uniform while he committed the crime in complete defiance to his parents and "the system." He had no shame in what he did. He scared the store employees and threatened them and, when he was caught, he told police he did not care about the victims in the store, or what the police or his parents thought about him. He felt he was far above the law and mused that he was invincible. Fairweather went as far as to tell the police that he considered killing the people inside the store but they weren't a challenge and he had better things to do.

In court for the armed robbery at the convenience store, the judge spoke to Fairweather about his troubling case and the facts of his unacceptable behavior. As the judge spoke, the child snickered at him in a completely disrespectful manner. Although the judge properly scolded the child in open court and *almost* remanded him into custody, he ultimately sentenced Fairweather to a 12-month referral order instead. It was determined that the child needed to have a counselor and should be closely monitored. However, this left a live wire free and able to do what he pleased. It was a decision, although arguably sound since Fairweather did not have a significant criminal history up to this point, that ended up costing two people their lives.

After Fairweather was apprehended (over a year after his first killing), he told police about the murder of James Attfield by stating, “I snuck out of the house through the living-room window.” Recall that he was basically on a time-out for twelve months, but remaining inside was not part of *his* ultimate plan. He told the investigators that he snuck out to find “a sacrifice,” and that he planned to kill someone in his home town. He never articulated why the person he wanted to kill had to be from his home town.

James only continued to say that voices told him he needed to be a killer; however, many glaring factors would be discovered sometime later about the boy that would convince the lay person that this kid needed to be in custody. He continued to try to convince those in law enforcement that interviewed him that if he did not kill someone -- and make a sacrifice to the voices in his head -- the voices would come and kill him.

Fairweather added, "I couldn't find no one. I then saw James Attfield lying there on the grass." Even at the age of fifteen, Fairweather had seen quite a bit in his life. He looked at James Attfield asleep in the grass and assumed because he was passed out that he was drunk. The fact Fairweather assumed James was drunk and he could see James Attfield was sound asleep convinced him that James was an easy target.

Fairweather later rationalized that James Attfield would never know he was about to be murdered until it was too late, and since he was asleep, he could not defend himself. The voices grew louder in his head and cheered him on to kill the man in the grass. Fairweather discussed how he was anxious to get his first real-life kill. This is a reference to first-person shooter video games. Based on what is available in regards to this case and James Fairweather, I don't think even he was prepared for what he was about to do next. One thing was certain, his mind was made up and there was no stopping him now.

Using the cover of darkness from the early morning hours, Fairweather slowly moved toward Attfield to ensure he would not alert or awaken the man. When he was approximately five feet from Attfield, he stopped and stared at him for some time. He did not immediately attack. The voices in his head erupted as the majority of them told him to kill the man immediately, to make the sacrifice they were all desperate to have. Another voice, one he rarely listened to, attempted to convince him that he should not murder the man just steps away from him. Yet another voice, one he repressed almost instantly, told James Fairweather there was still time to walk away. Tragically, Fairweather sided with the psychotic voices blaring in his skull; he jumped on top of James and violently brought his knife into the man's stomach. The ordeal would not be quick.

Fairweather later recalled about the event, "So I started stabbing, one shot missed and went into his eye and I went into a rage. There was a big pool of blood." This single statement, made by a child, caused the hair on the back of my neck to stand straight up. The cool and calm manner in which this kid speaks of taking a person's life should cause great concern for anyone who's within arm's reach of him. This statement alone convinces me that we have not heard the last of James Fairweather. It's possible, even though he's been sentenced, that he may eventually see life outside a prison. If that happens, he will be free to do whatever he pleases.

No one called for help and no one stepped in to rescue James Attfield. Fairweather proceeded to maliciously attack James for almost two minutes. He repeatedly stabbed James in the face and upper body. Attfield, as James Fairweather had said all along, never stood a chance of surviving the brutal knife assault.

Once Fairweather was confident his prey was dead, and the menacing voices simmered down in his head, he pushed himself off of James and stood up. He then stood over James's body and reveled in the carnage he caused with his own bloody hands. His mind tried to process real from fake as all the gory violence he'd seen in video games distorted his mental processing filters. It was clear, however, that what he'd just done was no video game. There was a dead man covered in blood at his feet to prove it.

After a few moments, Fairweather casually walked away from the crime scene as though nothing had happened -- as if he did not just use a knife to take another man's life. The voices within him died down almost completely, and James found himself internally at peace -- a feeling he hadn't felt since he was six or seven years old. We later learn that he took steps while leaving the scene to cover up this murder (we'll discuss them later).

The fact he killed a man, the manner in which he did so, and the way he acted after murdering James indicated without a doubt that James Fairweather was completely lost at this point. One could argue that the person who killed James Attfield was no longer James Fairweather the growing boy, but rather just a shell of a once normal child residing in a serial killer's body. We will later see that Fairweather "got off" by killing James and the possibility of killing others.

At approximately 6 a.m., a passerby noticed James Attfield in the grass in a pool of his own blood and frantically called the police. Paramedics got to the location first, quickly assessed the patient, and attempted to save James. Despite their diligent efforts, the patient had lost too much blood, and they were not able to save him. In all reality, James was dead before the paramedics even arrived. His passing, and the manner in which he was taken from his family and friends, was a tragic and terrible loss for the entire Colchester community.

Essex Police arrived to the reported homicide scene quickly. It had been awhile since a murder had happened in town and the police were curious as to what happened in this incident. The experienced law enforcement members quickly surveyed the scene. They could see the victim was stabbed repeatedly, although by what was not immediately clear. It was apparent whoever killed the victim had gone into a fit of rage. Essex Police detectives were summoned to the scene, they responded shortly thereafter, and began combing the murder scene for clues, evidence, or leads.

The overwhelming sight of the crime scene, consisting primarily of pools of blood and significant damage to the victim's head and upper torso, shocked hardened police officers. Bone and brain matter belonging to the victim were exposed -- a scene no one wants to process. The details of the attack and murder were not released to the public right away. In fact, the BBC determined at the time that the specific details were "too gruesome to describe." BBC officials did not report what they knew of the gory details of the murder to the public because they were concerned it might put everyone in a panic.

James Fairweather would later act out what he did to James Attfield while he was interviewed by Essex investigators. You can view the videos of his reenactment online. I've interviewed killers and truly terrible criminals in my career. Without a doubt, James Fairweather is among the worst human beings I've ever seen. He made me cringe as he relived his account of what he did to James Attfield. No one should ever meet the fate James Attfield met when stumbled upon by James Fairweather. When the investigators watched in awe as Fairweather confessed to stabbing his victim, Fairweather would describe the incident in a cold and emotionless manner. One investigator asked James, "What did you do next?"

"I stabbed him first there," Fairweather said as he touched his own stomach.

"And I done it a few times."

Fairweather added, "When I was doing that, my voices were laughing and laughing and laughing, louder and louder."

Think about these statements. Consider the fact that they came from a child easily discussing how he murdered a person in cold blood for nothing more than to allegedly appease voices in his head. It's bizarre and disturbing.

Originally, there were no leads in the murder of James Attfield. An interesting fact since the crime lasted over two minutes and occurred in an area that was not desolate or off-the-beaten-path. I cannot imagine someone did not see the killer straddling the victim and raising his arms up and down with a knife in his hands over one hundred times. And what of the sounds that had to have been made by the victim and likely the suspect as the crime unfolded? I cannot understand how allegedly no one saw the murder take place. Equally frustrating is that if someone did see the murder take place, they never came forward.

Evidence at the scene suggested the killer stabbed the victim at least 102 times, mostly in the victim's eyes and face, leading the investigators and the medical examiner to believe the crime was an extreme overkill and committed by a highly destructive individual. Many of the law enforcement people at the murder site had witnessed disgusting crime scenes before, but the images at this one, combined with the fact that the victim was later determined to have disabilities and the father of five children, were clearly disheartening to everyone involved. No one at the crime scene ever considered at the time that the killer would end up being a child...or that this child would end up being a serial killer.

The murder of James Attfield stunned the Colchester community... it would remain unsolved for over a year. Every aspect of the case caused great concern for local residents. Compounding issues was the fact that the police did not have answers for the public right away. However, the lack of answers for the public was not due to the lack of effort by local law enforcement. Just like everyone else touched by the case, local law enforcement wanted to identify and apprehend James Attfield's murderer.

Over seventy local criminals with criminal history involving a knife were questioned by Essex Police. Within that massive group of law breakers was James Fairweather, a minor. At the time, it was observed that Fairweather was "just a child," and he gave police an alibi that he was home during the time the crime was committed. It was noted that Fairweather was on a 12-month referral and it was assumed he would have been inside his home as he said he had been. In addition, Fairweather was convincing and very manipulative. It seems many serial killers can convince people they are telling the truth when they are not. Nevertheless, Essex police did not verify or corroborate Fairfield's alibi, and he was let go. This was a costly mistake.

From the date of the crime and up to January of 2015, over 900 persons of interest and possible witnesses to James Attfield's murder were interviewed and questioned by Essex Police. Police were hopeful that they could develop a lead in the high-profile case, but it seemed every person they questioned led to a dead end.

Detective Superintendent Hawkings, Head of Major Crimes for Essex Police, called the attack on James Attfield "brazen" since it occurred in a public space where passersby were likely. He noted that, despite little evidence being located at the crime scene, police considered that the attack could have been a hate crime (since James had a disability). However, the killer himself would later admit that James was selected completely randomly and that he did not know James Attfield prior to killing him. After the case was open to the public, Hawkings admitted that James Fairweather had always been a "person of interest" in the murder of James Attfield, but he added that they had no evidence connecting him to the scene.

Based on the severity of the crime and the fact police had no leads or possible suspects at the time, Colchester residents grew impatient and more fearful. Fewer local residents ventured outside because none of them wanted to meet the same demise as Mr. Attfield. Several months would pass before folks slowly began to walk around more freely. Oddly, right around the time people began to let their guard down, another murder, equally disturbing and savage, would take place.

Since James Attfield's body was found near overgrowth, police requested all of the overgrowth in the town be removed "to take away any hiding places for the unknown killer." The overgrowth throughout the town was removed, but we later learned that there were many more hiding places for James Fairweather. The one hiding place no one considered, and the one the killer chose while stalking and pouncing on his next victim, included him hiding in plain sight.

Chapter Two: A Serial Killer is Born?

Colchester, Essex – When was he born?

James Fairweather

James Fairweather as he looked when he was apprehended.

James Fairweather was born to Mr. James Fairweather (Senior) and Anita Fairweather in Colchester, Essex. According to available records, his mother, Anita Fairweather, is employed as a nurse. One source quoted that she also moonlights as a part-time worker at McDonald's. His father was a cleaner at Colchester United FC. Those who know James Fairweather Senior describe him as "down to Earth," a hard worker, and personable. Those who know Anita Fairweather describe her as loving and caring, perfect for her nursing profession. The arrest of her son and his subsequent murder charges has been particularly difficult for Anita.

By all accounts, young James Fairweather had a normal early adolescence and he was raised in a happy and loving home. At about the age of six, he began playing darts with his father and the two would play together often. A local dart player described the eventual serial killer as "quiet as a church mouse." Perhaps even at the age of six, the wheels in James's head were churning quickly and he held more conversations within his mind than outwardly with people that he came into contact with.

Details about his childhood will continue to emerge, but I managed to unearth more facts about James when he was between the ages of six and twelve and up to the point of his current age. School officials and friends described him as a "normal shy boy" who was "quiet, well-behaved, hardworking, kind, and sensitive to the needs of others." However, despite these initial assessments of James, things would take a drastic turn when he experienced tremendous sorrow and heartache. He was twelve years old at the time.

In April of 2012, James's Nan (grandmother) passed away from cancer. Her passing totally crushed him. He would discuss her passing with various psychiatrists while being interviewed regarding the murders of James Attfield and Nahid Almanea. One of the doctors noted about James's relationship with his grandmother, "He believed that she was a good person who shouldn't be taken away." I think most of us can recall our grandmothers, how kind and sweet they always were/are to us. Losing someone who treats you so well and who loves you deeply is difficult to handle at any age, but particularly rough when you are young.

The report noted that James was becoming angrier by the day and predicted that he would begin finding trouble while he transitioned to secondary school. Shortly thereafter, James was taken to the school office one morning after he head-butted a child and kicked another during a playground scuffle. Another report surfaced concluding that James was becoming more abrasive and a real handful for school officials. One of his teachers also mentioned that James often had verbal arguments with his parents and he constantly told people no one knew what he was dealing with.

Local newspapers sought a spin for the case of James Fairweather because, once it became known that he was fifteen years old and a serial killer, people in the community were outraged and perplexed. The media searched for anyone who claimed to know James Fairweather, especially when the court allowed his name and identity to be released after convicting him of two murders. His name was unknown up until that point because he was a minor.

In one story, a schoolgirl attending Colchester Academy alleged, "A teacher asked him (James Fairweather) what he wanted to do when he was older, and he said, 'I want to be a murderer'. Just before his Year 11 final assembly, he said he was going to come in and shoot everyone." How his behavior and comments were not alarming to those around James Fairweather is shocking to me. It's unclear what, if anything, was done after James made these terrifying statements.

School records indicate and confirm that James was found guilty of robbing a local convenience store but was allowed to return to school. This child, who was clearly losing his mind and becoming progressively worse, returned to school just a few days after he used a knife to hold up a convenience store. It was the same school that he had threatened to destroy in a "Columbine-like" incident. Officials isolated James and allowed him back on campus because he needed to complete his exams. Alone, in a room with a proctor and his demented thoughts, James haphazardly took the test with no interest in passing it. He had far greater plans for himself than continuing in school.

The secondary school he attended is known as Colchester Academy. While there, the kids took every opportunity they had to tease and bully him about his large ears. As a result, he got into several physical altercations. Most boys do in some fashion or the other at that age, right? According to school records, he did not receive high grades and he was placed in the "lower sets" in each of the classes he was enrolled in. At one point in his academic career, many of the teachers had already written him off. It seems James needed help academically and he struggled to fit in. In addition, it was confirmed that he actually told a teacher who asked him what he wanted to be when he grew up that he wanted to be "a murderer." I would not have found the comment to be funny and I would have reported it to the police.

Several of the students in his class pushed him further about his claim of wanting to be a murderer, and he told them he was going to come back and execute a "Columbine-like" incident at the school. He said he had guns and knives. He even told his schoolmates that he was planning to do it at the school's final assembly. Nevertheless, the students and school staff apparently blew James off, as usual, and it does not appear any of his outlandish statements were reported to local law enforcement. Once again, the lack of disclosure of such inflammatory statements to the police contributed to why James remained free to kill.

In the United States, California specifically, we have school resource officers on many of our school campuses. I know all of the School Resource Officers at my office. None of them would have turned a blind eye to a comment like this from a clearly disturbed and angry teenager. Therefore, I believe local police were never aware that James Fairweather was self-destructing and intent on taking as many people as he could with him.

Chapter Three: The Murder of Nahid Almanea

Colchester, Essex, Salary Brook Trail, June 17, 2014

Nahid Almanea, murdered by James Fairweather.

University of Essex student Nahid Almanea, aged 31, walked along the Salary Brook Trail close to her home. She wore a full-length Muslim robe, a Hijab (a traditional scarf), and sunglasses. We can only speculate as to what she thought while she walked, but her friends and family described her as loving, gentle, and kind, so I choose to believe she was full of happy thoughts as she strolled along.

The registrar at Essex University, Bryn Morris, later said of Almanea, "Nahid was a bright, talented and conscientious member of our university community. She was a considerate and well-respected student in our English-language program and is missed by her teachers and fellow students.

"We will continue to honor her memory through the Almanea scholarship for science, which is offered to overseas students studying science or health-related subjects at postgraduate level."

Without a doubt, Nahid Almanea was well respected and clearly had her entire life ahead of her. Not a single person could utter a disparaging comment about Nahid Almanea. It's clear she'd set a course to be successful, but none of her careful planning and sacrifices could have saved her once a serial killer spotted her walking along Salary Brook Trail. This killer, only a child, began to stalk her in plain sight, and she had no idea he was behind her and plotting how to end her life.

James Fairweather later told police that he was in the area looking to pacify the voices in his head that had ordered him to kill ... again. The voices, according to James, said they would come for him if he did not make another sacrifice like the one he made when he murdered James Attfield.

Scanning the surrounding area, James hatched a plan to murder a woman he saw walking only a few yards in front of him. It appears (at least based on the records I was able to obtain) that there was no one else on the trail besides James Fairweather and Nahid Almanea. This seems strange because it was broad daylight and in an area frequently used by residents and students to walk to the university and around town.

James crept up behind Nahid, reached around her before she could react, and stabbed her with a bayonet in the stomach.

Nahid fell to the ground and James jumped on top of her. She fought with him and tried to defend herself from her crazed attacker. He slapped her sunglasses off her face so he could stab her in both of her eyes. James drove the knife through her orbital sockets and into her brain. He later said he did this to ensure the woman "could not see evil." Those who study serial killers might recall that Peter Sutcliffe did the same with one of his victims, and some later argued that Fairweather did what he did to pay homage to Sutcliffe. Regardless of the reason, the completely disturbing act signified just how far gone teenager James Fairweather was.

As he'd done after killing James Attfield, James Fairweather pushed himself off of Nahid and walked away as though nothing had happened. He was able to leave the area and make it home without anyone speaking to him or noticing that he was covered in blood. James continued to re-live the act of taking Nahid's life over and over in his head. He felt a tremendous rush knowing that he was in complete control of Nahid. After he got home, he hid some of his clothes, took a shower to clean himself, and turned to playing violent video games.

About an hour later, a walker on the trail where the attack and murder occurred, discovered Nahid in a pool of blood and called the police. Essex Police and paramedics responded to the scene quickly but they were unable to save Nahid. Police knew right away, based on the evidence at the scene (she'd obviously not suffered an accident and her body bore numerous puncture wounds), that the victim had been murdered and assumed she'd been killed with a knife or other similar sharp object. Because the victim was wearing traditional Muslim clothing, police originally felt that she might have been murdered in some sort of hate-crime event. Police would stay focused on the hate-crime angle for quite some time. Still, no matter why Nahid was murdered, law enforcement was determined to find her killer. They could not have known at the time that Nahid's murder was related to James Attfield's murder.

Fairweather would later describe the subtleties of how he killed Nahid: "I went behind her and the voices started laughing, I remember again they were really, really loud."

In a calm and controlled voice James continued, "She [Nahid] stumbled and I hit her in the eye, the third blow I popped her in the eye and I went into a rage again. They were laughing in my head, going, "You did it." In this statement, when James speaks the words, "I went into a rage again," he was referring to exactly what he did to James Attfield. He never tried to hide what he'd done to Nahid or James. In fact, he seemed to enjoy the attention and reveled in the death and destruction he'd caused.

Detectives asked James about the victim's (Nahid's) sunglasses and he replied, "I knocked them off so I could stab her in the eye." When asked if he killed her because she was Muslim, James answered, "No, she was a sinner, a sacrifice."

The similarities between the deaths of James Attfield and Nahid Almanea stunned the Colchester and Essex community. Some people recalled that James Attfield was murdered in an area close to where Nahid had been killed, and both victims were stabbed to death. The discussion about a possible serial killer being on the loose did not occur, however. The two victims (male versus female, white versus Saudi Arabian, time of day of the killings) were so different and the attacks seemed so random that police did not consider them the work of a serial killer.

Detective Constable Jane Morgan, a family liaison between Essex Police and the Nahid Family, read a statement from her family shortly after her death that read, “As a family we have been left devastated by the terrible murder of Nahid. Nahid was a remarkable and gentle person who was loved for her kind and caring nature.

“Publicly, Nahid was a quiet and dignified lady who chose to pursue her academic studies in order to work towards her PhD, and whilst in England she made a decision that she would respect her heritage and traditions in the way that she dressed and conducted herself.

“However, when she was with her family, Nahid was a warm and loving person who enjoyed laughter and the company of her parents, siblings and extended family. The amount of people that attended Nahid’s funeral is a tribute to how much she was cared for and respected.”

Police were hopeful that this heartfelt message would strike a nerve with anyone who might have witnessed her murder to come forward. However, no one stepped up to say they'd seen anything related to Nahid's murder. (There is the possibility that no one actually witnessed the event, but this is highly unlikely.)

As I said of the circumstances of James Attfield's murder, it does not seem even remotely possible that not a single person saw any portion of James Fairweather's senseless attack on Nahid. The motions and sounds happening during the struggle would catch anyone's eye as they strolled along the path. Perhaps my career has made me overly skeptical, but the fact that no one allegedly saw James Fairweather kill Nahid Almanea continues to bother me.

A terrible part of Nahid's murder was the fact it might not have happened at all if she had been walking with her brother, Raed Almanea, who attended Essex University with her and normally walked with her to classes. Raed would blame himself for not being able to save his sister, but it clearly was never his fault. Fate, as it normally does, struck and left behind tragedy.

Raed Almanea told Essex Police after the shock wore off about his sister, "I was full of optimism but came back in the evening full of grief and sorrow." I don't have siblings, but the fact Raed and Nahid were attending the same college, it seems they would have been very close. Although he'd blame himself for her attack, the fact remained that a serial killer had locked eyes on Nahid and she had no idea she was being stalked and would later fall to the voices inside the mind of a child who was also a murderer.

Nevertheless, the investigation continued. Essex Police, stuck with no leads or potential suspect(s), were forced to release some of the evidence they had with regard to Nahid's attack in order to see if anyone in the community could/would help. In any murder investigation, evidence is highly guarded and usually is not released. Doing so is sometimes frowned upon, but law enforcement members involved in the case were desperate, and desperate times force desperate decisions.

Video surveillance of the attacker stalking Nahid along the trail was released to newspapers and the media. Although the lighting of the video was poor and the image was grainy, detectives hoped someone would recognize the unknown male figure who they said killed Nahid. The video showed a medium height and medium built male wearing large or baggy clothing apparently following Nahid. After the video was released, calls came in to police and the leads were chased, but ultimately police were no closer to identifying the suspect after releasing the video.

During the same time, Essex Police once again found and briefly interviewed James Fairweather. They noted that the child had a criminal charge for a robbery in which he used a knife during the crime and that he'd been interviewed regarding the murder of James Attfield. Just as he'd done when he was questioned about James Attfield, James Fairweather convinced the police he was home during the time Nahid Almanea was killed. And, just as before, the police let James Fairweather go. Although this time, James was considered a strong person of interest in both murders, which meant police would be watching him closely. Unbelievably, he was not observed closely enough as he almost struck a third time.

Investigators search the trail for evidence.

Police search for clues in the murder of Nahid Almanea.

Chapter Four: Thwarting a Serial Killer's Plans

Colchester, Essex, May 27, 2015

Michelle Sadler, James Fairweather's intended third victim and the person responsible for his apprehension.

Michelle Sadler, a local Colchester woman, walked her dog along a path near to where Nahid Almanea had been murdered in the mid-morning hour. Something along the overgrowth caught her attention.

A male teenager, wearing a combat jacket she thought she'd heard the police warn her about (mentioned by police as possibly what the killer wore when he killed Nahid and was slightly visible in the surveillance footage they'd released), stared at her as she walked by him. Michelle noticed the male teenager was also wearing a pair of gloves and was "lurking in the bushes." She thought it strange that he did not speak to her and he wore gloves for no apparent reason. She noted it was not cold and it did not appear the boy was working.

Based on what Michelle knew of the murder of Nahid Almanea and James Attfield, and the fact the teenager appeared to be lying in wait along a similar path as to where Nahid had been killed, Michelle began to get nervous and fearful for her own safety.

In Michelle's own words, "I walk my dog close to the nature trail and was down there on my own. I saw him hiding in the bushes and looking really suspicious. I nearly shit myself when I saw him there." She paused then added, "When I close my eyes I see his face. I see those thick black glasses staring back at me."

She explained how she thought about getting away but she didn't want to leave another dog walker in harm's way, "He was so odd looking, I turned and left making sure he wasn't following me, stepping up my pace with every step. I saw another dog walker and told her I was calling the police. She said she had a big dog and said we should check out what he was up to. I convinced myself to go back because I would never forgive myself if something happened."

"He was nowhere to be seen, then the lady said 'Look, he's there,' and I turned and saw him hiding in the bushes."

"He was no more than 15 feet away and staring straight at me. It's a face that will never leave me, a manic look. Just as I grabbed the woman by the arm and said, 'We have to get out of here', I noticed his jacket. It was the same jacket I had seen in the papers, that police said one of the killers was wearing. I was shaking, so I called police."

Michelle, moments prior simply walking her dog, was now face to face with an unbelievably sick serial killer. Thankfully she was able to phone the police and they responded as fast as they could. Essex police officers located James exactly as Michelle had described, lurking in some bushes wearing surgical gloves. They moved in and were able to handcuff him. In his jacket pocket, they found the knife pictured below.

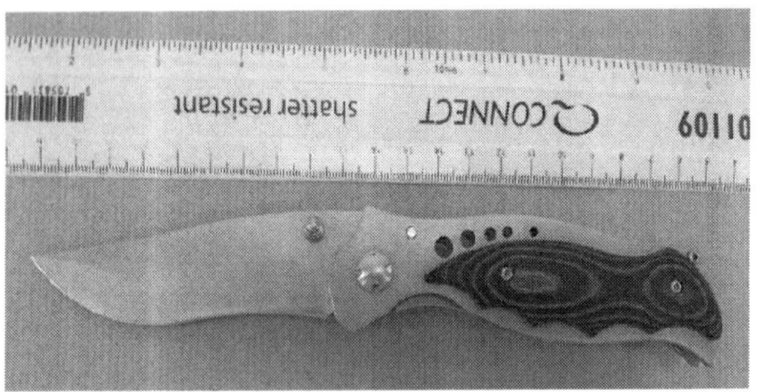

The knife James had on him when he was arrested.

James Fairweather did not resist the police when they handcuffed him and he appeared almost happy to see them. According to court documents, James said to them during his arrest, "I'm waiting for someone to kill." Before the officers could say anything, he added, "I've done it twice before."

The officers placed James in a patrol car and drove him to the Essex Police Station. While there, they phoned his mother, Anita Fairweather, and asked her to come to the station to sit with James while they interviewed him. They did not tell her that he was the prime suspect in the murders of James Attfield and Nahid Almanea.

Anita responded to the police station, scared and gravely concerned for her son and what he may have done, and the investigation began to finally take shape, some fourteen months after James Attfield was murdered.

As a result of James's statements he made during his questioning, he was charged with two murders and remanded into custody. This was only a small step in this case as a lengthy investigation was left after James had confessed.

The following is the transcript of the 999 call (equivalent of 911 in the States) Michelle placed when she noticed James Fairweather lurking in some overgrowth:

Tuesday, May 26, 2015

Operator: "Essex Police Control Room"

Caller: "Hi, I wonder if you can help me. I'm actually on the Salary Brook erm the Longridge end of the trail where that murder was last year and there's a very suspicious guy down there who's just standing there, and it's like obviously a dog trail and he's just on his own and it's quite a secluded area. Erm I don't think there's anyone around to have a look and he's got like a, I don't know, could be wrong but he's got..."

Operator: "Right."

Caller: "...a jacket that looks very similar to what was all over the paper and everything and it's on the same trail as what happened err almost a year ago."

Operator: "Okay."

Caller: "Yeah."

Operator: "What's suspicious about him?"

Caller: "Well to be honest with you he's on a bridge huh and yeah not a footpath..."

Unknown female: (Indecipherable speech)

Caller: "...yeah he was stood behind some of the trees and there's it's obviously it's only like a dog (inaudible) place. And I first went down on my own with my dog and I saw him sort of hiding.."

Operator: "Mm."

Caller: "..and it made me freeze..."

Operator: "Did you..."

Caller: "...thinking he'll come out."

Operator: "..is he in a bush did you say sort of hiding?"

Caller: "No he's practically he's hiding, he's practically, he's on a bridge just practically yeah he's sec, in a secluded area he's not in the main bit and then I've come out with one of the other ladies that's got a big dog and we've walked down there and he's a little bit further into the bushes a little bit and...."

Operator: "Right"

Caller:" ...yeah..."

Operator: "Yeah."

Caller: "..and it's just like not the sort of person, person..."

Operator: "So Salary on the ..."

Caller:" ..you expect to see someone."

Operator: "...bridge in bushes?"

Caller: "Yeah it's yeah it's just and he's got thick dark glasses I don't if that makes, I don't know it's just something's not right."

Operator: "Okay."

Caller: "Clearly not right."

Operator: "Where did you say this was?"

Caller: "Well it's on the, it's on the Salary Brook Trail."

Operator: "Salary Brook..."

Caller: "And.."

Operator: ".. Trail?"

Unknown Female: "Okay (indecipherable speech).."

Caller: "Yeah it's the Longridge end of the Salary Brook Trail erm yeah so it's the little bridge that goes across into the Bowmans Ford."

Unknown female: (Inaudible)

Caller: "It's just there's, there's no you'd never see somebody down there that's all."

Operator: "Salary Brook Trail. I'm just looking for that location now. Is there, is any sort of buildings nearby that I can use as a reference point to put on my system?"

Shortly thereafter, Essex Police were dispatched to the area where Michelle had called from. They spotted James, made a safe approach, and apprehended him. By no means, though, were police done with their investigation. Next we'll discuss what police had done prior to the moment they apprehended James. From there we'll discuss all of the hard work they did after he confessed to killing two local residents.

Chapter Five: The Investigation into the murders of James Attfield and Nahid Almanea

Colchester, Essex, 2014/2015

Recall what we've already discussed regarding the work the Essex Police Department (and other local police departments) had done early on with regard to the murders of James Attfield and Nahid Almanea. Admittedly, their hands were full as they conducted a professional, tedious, and thorough investigation for both cases. The murders were not considered connected until much later, but many law enforcement members involved in both cases felt there could be a connection (although no one speculated specifically as to what the connection might be...more of a hunch if you will).

These "hunches" have tormented me throughout my seventeen-year career; they don't always pan out and can be very misleading. As an investigator and detective,

I chased the evidence because it's what I would use to seek a conviction on the suspect. Sometimes, the evidence doesn't exist. I'd spend time trying to figure out patterns or draw upon my experiences to steer me in the right direction. For example, when I was chasing murder suspects on the run, all kinds of information about the suspect would flood the command center. Everyone saw something or knows someone who might be able to assist law enforcement. Sorting through the leads would take days, but when a suspect was making a run to Mexico, I had hours, not days. A specific feeling -- a hunch -- would present itself and my team and I would follow it. We were extremely successful, but there were times I spent twelve hours in the wrong part of town on a bad hunch.

The following is a chronological order of how things played out for the James Fairweather investigation.

June 24, 2014

After Nahid's murder, an appeal was issued by Essex detectives intended for a man who they thought followed Nahid approximately four days prior to her murder. They said several witnesses noticed this man walking behind two women near 8:45 a.m. on June 13, 2014, a Friday. The witnesses thought one of the two women, based on her physical size and her outfit, could have been Nahid. Police noted that both women had exited a house on Stanley Wooster Way, Colchester.

A sketch was released that depicted the man as being in his thirties, white, around 5ft 10in tall, and with short, dark hair. The man was dressed casually and wore dark blue jeans. Some of the witnesses said the man spoke with a local Colchester accent.

We later learn that the true suspect was nothing like the man described in the original police sketch. Chasing false or inaccurate leads bogs down investigations, especially murder investigations, and causes law enforcement to become frustrated. Nevertheless, every lead needs to be sniffed out because you never know if it will lead you to your suspect. The police force in this case, based on the sketch, thought their suspect was a grown adult and roamed the city looking for someone similar to the person depicted in the sketch. Someone like

James Fairweather -- slight and a child -- could be completely dismissed because he looked nothing like the information provided from a witness.

Steve Worron, Assistant Chief Constable, pleaded with the people of Colchester, "People living and working in the local area are the key to helping us find whoever killed this bright, young woman who was a guest in our country. The answers lie in the local community and we will find whoever did this. So far the support we have had from the public has been great. Every time we issue an appeal, we have a surge of information coming through into our incident room." Some calls came in after this appeal, but no one recognized the man from the sketch.

A few days later, another angle was chased by the detectives. They noted that a cycling couple, a man and a woman, were close to Nahid's crime scene around 10:45 a.m. on June 17, 2015. The cyclists were described as being in their early twenties and were traveling on Salary Brook Trail in the direction of Greenstead Estate.

The police said the male rider had dark hair, was tall and slim, and had olive-colored skin while the woman was wearing a "flowing pattern tiered shirt" and she had long dark hair. Again, although the appeal by police was strong, no one came forward to say they were the bicyclists or that they knew who the bicyclists were.

At this point in the investigation, it's estimated that over one hundred police officers from Kent, Metropolitan Police, and Essex Police were working the murders of Nahid Almanea and James Attfield. In addition, profilers from the National Crime Agency had joined the case and pored over every bit of evidence and case notes from both crime scenes hoping to identify a possible killer or killers. None of the weapons used for the killings had been located yet, and the idea of a serial killer being involved still had not taken shape.

Every stone and bush was kicked by investigators scouring the area for evidence or clues. A fishing pond near where Nahid had been found was drained and police actually went into the water and conducted an "intensive fingertip search." This means they bent down in the remaining water and used their fingers to massage the pond bottom full of mud and sludge hoping to find a murder weapon or evidence. Sadly, their efforts were met with negative results.

The final two potential leads police had were two men seen in the area of Nahid's murder around the time she was believed to have been killed.

The first man, seen wearing a "distinctive beige-colored jacket" while walking along Salary Brook Trail around the time of the attack, was described as being between his late teens and early thirties, of average height and build, tanned, and having "thick, black hair in a two-to-three-inch mop style on top." This person was seen walking in the direction of the Greenstead Estate between 10:20 a.m. and 10:40 a.m.

The second man was described as being between the ages of eighteen and twenty-five, with dark hair, and a medium build. This person was seen "running up Hewes Close at about 10:56 a.m." One witness said the man was wearing a "long-sleeved, plain London Bus red hooded top and dark trousers." As with so many of the potential leads in the murders of James

Attfield and Nahid Almanea, no one came forward to say they were the person of the appeal or that they knew who the people were in the appeal. Every officer and detective involved in the case was exhausted and felt as though they would never crack this case. Frustration boiled over into the community as people asked if it was safe to go outside.

January 2015

As the investigation stretched to January of 2015, police were beginning to think they may never identify the killer(s) in this case. According to available records, police estimated that they had interviewed over 900 people for the case, and yet no significant leads were made.

Detective Superintendent Tracy Hawkings, Head of Major Crimes for Essex, was very outspoken regarding both attacks. She called the attacks "brazen" and noted that the attacks occurred in a public space "where passersby were likely." A common theme told by the police was that, even though they had little evidence, they felt strongly that Nahid's murder was a hate crime. With nothing to shift this line of thinking, I don't see any issues with police looking for suspect(s) who were known to be racist.

Much later, though, we learned that one person killed both victims and racism had nothing to do with the killings. Prematurely assuming Nahid's murder was a hate crime led the Islamic State of Iraq and the Levant (ISIL) to threaten revenge attacks, using the Twitter hashtag #Colchester. It's unclear who exactly ISIL would have targeted in their alleged retaliation attacks, but their involvement (and very public acknowledgment) in Nahid's case demonstrates how huge the case had grown.

The fact that Nahid Almanea and James Attfield were unconnected people, and had been killed at different times of the day, led to a line of investigation by local police that there might have been two separate killers. Whether there was one or two (or more) killers involved, the sentiment around town was that people were afraid. Fewer people went outside in Colchester, and overgrowth around the city was cleared to remove hiding places.

The moment James Fairweather was apprehended

The investigation into the murders of James Attfield and Nahid Almanea, one of the biggest in the history of Essex, cost £2.6 million (3.7 million US dollars). This is an extremely high sum, but these murders -- in this case serial murders -- always cost a lot of money. No one would argue about paying such a large amount of money. You cannot place a monetary value on the lives of Nahid Almanea and James Attfield.

At one point, it's estimated that close to 1,500 officers and support staff from the Metropolitan Police, Kent, and Essex Police were involved in the investigation of James Attfield's and Nahid Almanea's murders. One of the reasons so many officers were involved was that law enforcement felt the large increase in police presence would help calm some of the residents while they tried to identify and capture a murderer.

As we know, the call from Michelle Sadler and the quick response by Essex Police landed James Fairweather into custody. His willingness to talk openly about what he'd done forced the case into overdrive -- he confessed, explained how and why he killed, and told police where to look for evidence -- and police had to hustle to certain places to find murder weapons that James had stashed after he killed Mr. Attfield and Ms. Almanea. Immediately after Fairweather confessed to killing James Attfield and Nahid Almanea, he was charged with their murders, and he would remain in custody for the trial.

After he was apprehended, law enforcement learned numerous scary things about James Fairweather. He told police that he was "turned on" by serial killers. He showed them where he had researched Myra Hindley, Ian Huntley, and the Yorkshire Ripper. He proudly showed the investigators his favorite photo on his phone; it was a picture of serial killer Peter Sutcliffe. Finally, he boasted that his favorite serial killer was American Ted Bundy, an infamous serial killer known for sexually assaulting, murdering, and decapitating his victims.

James Fairweather did not stop there while sharing his insatiable fantasies about serial killers with the investigators, who by now had their own jaws in their hands, unable to comprehend the things coming from a child's mouth. He told police that he was planning to kill his parents, the head teacher of his school, and one of the officers in the station. The investigators asked him which officer? James grinned and pointed at the officer who was busy getting him a glass of water.

One interesting point that later came out in his trial, which I find completely spooky, was the fact that Fairweather said he was inspired to kill people based on playing computer and video games. He constantly played "Call of Duty" and "Grand Theft Auto" beginning at the age of thirteen. His parents, like the majority of the parents would have done, waited to let their son play such games until he was thirteen years old; they had no idea the games would influence him so much. The makers of these games make billions of dollars a year and have put warnings (that the graphics are adult-rated and the gaming sensation while playing could cause seizures) on the games since they were released.

I've played both games and I don't allow my own children to play them ... yet. However, they've seen and played them anyway. The games are in fact gory and almost too realistic. If the player jumps on to the internet, even more possibilities exist (such as being added to private parties or internet stalkers trying to lure our children). I'm not prepared to slap the blame in this case squarely on the gaming industry, but given the statements made by a known child serial killer about these sorts of games, we must at least admit that they could contribute to the making of a serial killer.

Fairweather also had another passion, that of horror movies and films. His parents located several horror movies in his room including Wrong Turn: The Carnage Collection, a DVD about Peter Sutcliffe, and a book called *The World's Worst Crimes*. Once again, these movies and books, full of violence, dismemberment, the bizarre, and death, impacted Fairweather deeply. He would watch these movies over and over, get excited, and fantasize about doing what he saw the villains doing in the movies. These movies and books, ones he should not have been in possession of, contributed to him decriminalizing illegal behavior (and his own behavior) and helped him justify his twisted thoughts.

In addition, we later learned that Fairweather was infatuated with pornography. He specifically liked "hard porn," which typically showed women being sexually brutalized and treated despicably by men (and sometimes by other women). The scenes were not of lovemaking or of couples being gentle, but rather they were filled with scenes of women being beaten, gagged, tied up, whipped, and generally abused. Fairweather watched this type of pornography as often as he could. Repeatedly observing the disrespectful and dehumanizing acts forced upon the women in the videos changed him as well. He desensitized the horrific acts being done on women and he began to think what he was watching was "the norm."

Lastly, the investigators were made aware of the fact that Fairweather was obsessed with his killings and would scour the internet looking for and reading every single article or blurb mentioned about his dirty work. His browser history was inundated with searches about the murders and he bookmarked every single page. Fairweather would spend countless hours reading about the death and destruction he caused. He would get very excited, even sexually, and would sometimes fondle himself.

After his apprehension, Fairweather was interviewed at length by doctors and psychologists. Based on his age and the ease with which he spoke of killing people (and the fact he'd killed two people), specialists were eager to find out, if possible, what made a child turn into a serial killer.

Fairweather openly spoke of his childhood and began opening up about his life. He stated he was not fond of large groups of people and that he wet his bed until the age of eight years old. He told Dr. Philip Joseph, a consultant forensic psychiatrist, during one interview, "I was sitting in the classroom being bullied and all of a sudden I heard voices saying, 'Why are you taking this from these people?'"

The serial killer continued, "As time went by they got louder, more aggressive, saying violent things. I felt they were my friends and I distanced myself from other people. People called me a 'freak' and a 'weirdo' because I was talking to myself."

Fairweather elaborated on the voices he heard while speaking to Dr. Simon Hill, a consultant forensic psychologist who cared for him, “I thought the voices were coming from the devil. I didn't mention them to anyone because if I did they told me they would come and get me.” Based on these statements and numerous other similar statements, Dr. Simon Hill would later inform the court during Fairweather’s trial that his patient had the “most anti-social, violent thoughts” he had ever heard.

Dr. Hill testified that James told him the voices he heard ordered him (Fairweather) to set babies on fire and to cut their heads off. Dr. Hill added that his client told him that he watched violent pornographic movies prior to him hearing the voices that currently dominated his mind.

“He watched violent and pornographic films on his computer. He said he watched those films before the voices. But after hearing voices, the videos excited him,” Dr. Hill told the court.

Dr. Hill finished by stating, “He (Fairweather) admitted being turned on by the thought of serial killers, but his excitement increased after he started hearing voices.”

I'm not a doctor, but what I do possess is seventeen years of law enforcement experience. Every statement made by James Fairweather prior to the killings and after scares me. These statements should have bothered anyone who heard him speak. Whether he was making all of this stuff up or he truly believed what he said to several different officers, psychologists, and therapists, the red flags about this child heading in a very dangerous direction should have popped up immediately. Somehow, this child slipped through the cracks and the ultimate price was paid two times because of it.

We owe it to people like James Fairweather, and to ourselves, to do everything possible to prevent serial killers from gaining momentum and taking human life. Ultimately, James's head was wired incorrectly and a series of events unlocked an instinct to kill. Unlike the majority (if not all) of other serial killer cases I've written about, I believe this one could have been prevented. It may have been difficult to do so, but not impossible.

Inspectors responded to Primrose Walk to search a dog bin where James told them he had disposed of some of his clothing after he killed Nahid. Bloody clothing was located in the dog bin and would later be used against James during the trial.

Essex Police officers responded to Wivenhoe Trail to search for the knife and bayonet that James used to kill Mr. Attfield and Ms. Almanea. Just as James had told them, the bayonet and knife (crucial evidence in the case against James) were located, collected, and booked as evidence.

In September of 2015, forensic evidence in the form of DNA was located on the hands of Nahid. In her fingernails was skin with matching DNA to James Fairweather. Obviously this was a massive piece of evidence and connected James to her murder. This was important because he would later allege in court that he did not kill Nahid and that his confession was coerced by law enforcement.

Based on finding the bloody clothing, the initial statements and confession made by James Fairweather, the DNA located on Nahid that matched James, and the murder weapons being located, law enforcement presented their case to the Crown and a trial was set in the double murder case against teenager James Fairweather.

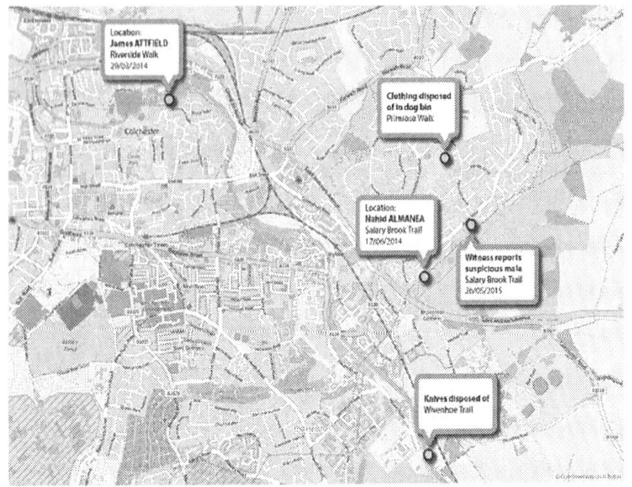

Significant mapping for the Attfield/Almanea murder cases.

Surveillance footage of James Fairweather leaving the murder scene of James Attfield.

Police search for evidence in the James Fairweather case.

Chapter Six: The Trial Against James Fairweather

Old Bailey Courthouse, January 3, 2016

The true name for "Old Bailey" is Central Criminal Court. Its local name comes from the street where the building stands, and criminal court cases in England and Wales are heard within its walls. A portion of the current building rests on the site of medieval Newgate gaol. Once a road named

Old Bailey followed the fortified walls of London and traveled from Ludgate Hill until meeting the junction of Holborn Viaduct and Newgate Street. It's an area rich in history and the location for a number of high-profile cases within the United Kingdom.

There are several buildings in the area. These buildings include the Crown Court. Normally major trials are held at the Crown Court and trials within Old Bailey are open to the public. As such, several security procedures are in place to prevent possible criminal activity.

As far as trials go, specifically with regard to those of a serial killer, James Fairweather's trial was rather "quick." He was arraigned on two capital murder charges in the beginning of January 2016, and by April 22, 2016, he was found guilty of killing James Attfield and Nahid Almanea.

There never was a shred of doubt that James Fairweather killed two people, but what he argued was that he did so while in an altered state of mind -- allegedly hearing the Devil himself -- and therefore he could not be found guilty by reason of diminished responsibility. In the United States, this type of defense is used often, but with the label of 'not guilty by reason of insanity.' It is a ploy that rarely works.

Among the facts that came out during the Fairweather trial was that James Fairweather has autism. His attorney attempted to call autism a disability and tried to beg for sympathy from everyone in the courtroom because his client had "a disability." It was discussed in court several times that James Attfield had a disability stemming from a car accident he was in. By bringing up autism, Fairweather's attorney was hoping the jury would be sympathetic toward his client. Until the trial, James and his family did not know James had a form of autism. This alone suggests James displayed very few signs of the disorder and was able to function rather well.

Autism, now known as "Autism spectrum disorder," is officially classified as a significant neurodevelopmental disorder. Typically, it will impair a child's ability to communicate and interact with others. In many cases, children will exhibit "restricted repetitive behaviors, interests, and activities." Most psychiatrists would argue that autism will also cause "impairment in social, occupational, and other areas of functioning."

It's unclear who diagnosed James with autism. But based on what I know of autism, my experience with children who have autism, and the research I've done regarding disorders and psychotic behavior over the last seventeen years, I feel confident in stating that James has a very minor form of autism.

In any event, the court heard testimony by two different doctors. They both agreed that being diagnosed with autism would not lead to someone being a cold-blooded killer. It was pointed out time and again that millions of kids have been diagnosed with autism and they aren't becoming serial killers. In the United States alone, more than 3.5 million people are diagnosed with autism. There is no available data or an established correlation between autism and serial killers, but most educated people would not support a connection between the two.

Another tactic used by James's attorney was informing the court that his client had "full-blown psychosis." Through his attorney, James tried to argue that he did not completely comprehend what he was doing when he killed James and Nahid. However, as with the argument about autism, prosecutor Philip Bennetts, QC, was able to prove that James knew exactly what he was doing at the time he stabbed two people to death. In addition, Mr. Bennetts argued that James was in complete control of himself when he deliberately took the lives of two people.

Mr. Bennetts, through officer, detective, and inspector testimony, was able to prove that James actually planned killing two people, and after he committed the murders, he "took steps to conceal afterwards." After killing Mr. Attfield, James threw the knife he used into the River Colne trying to get rid of the murder weapon. Someone who is "psychotic" would not have tried to cover up what they'd done.

The concept of James hearing voices, which came about from James himself, was also attacked by the prosecution team. Mr. Bennetts informed the court that James did not hear voices and made it all up. Two separate doctors, one employed by the court and one employed by Mr. Bennetts, felt

James was lying about having hallucinations and hearing voices. Both doctors felt James made it up because he thought he could get off murder charges by trying to act insane. Dr. Philip Joseph told the court that James's "description of hallucinations were clichéd and unconvincing." When prodded further by the trial judge about what he meant by this statement, Mr. Joseph added, "It seems more like something you might see in a horror film." In essence, Mr. Joseph felt James had watched a lot of horror movies and read a lot of crime books and used what he read and saw to formulate his story about hearing voices.

During the trial, James rarely showed emotion and seemed uninterested in the proceedings. He would be seen mouthing things to his mother, Anita, who attended every single court hearing. The presentation of evidence by both sides was methodical and efficient. Once the prosecution and defense rested their cases and made final closing arguments, the jury was asked to deliberate on what they'd heard for the last few months.

Eight hours and thirty-three minutes later, the jury advised Justice Robin Spencer that they had reached a verdict. James was brought back into the courtroom and listened as the jury found him -- in a unanimous vote -- guilty of two capital murders.

Anita Fairweather could not fight back tears and sobbed uncontrollably. James Senior held a stoic pose, but it was clear he was shaken. James Junior did not even flinch as the jury read their verdict. In fact, he mouthed something to the effect of him 'not giving a fuck' about the verdict or his looming sentencing hearing. The case, the fact the killer was a teenager, and every excruciating detail wore on the jury. Mr. Spencer excused the jurors from further service for a period of four years.

Although the guilty verdict was well-received, it would not bring back Nahid or James. The two families were happy with the results and were hopeful that they could begin to find closure for the terrible ordeal they'd been through over the last two years. They took comfort knowing the killer had been caught and was found guilty.

James Attfield's mother, Julie Finch, was very outspoken during this case. After the verdict was read, she could not hold back much of what she had been feeling for almost two years. She was quoted as saying, "James was a kind and brave son and he didn't deserve to die."

"At the time we had no idea the killer was so young – a fact that makes my son's death feel all the more cruel and unnecessary. James Fairweather is a monster in our eyes -- and we will never be able to forgive him."

While remaining strong, Julie thanked the media and local law enforcement for "their support and sensitivity throughout the investigation and trial."

*****

On April 29, 2016, James Fairweather and all of the people touched by his case came back to court to hear what his sentence would be. Justice Spencer started by stating directly to James, "I have no doubt that you acted out ... violent, sadistic fantasies fueled by your obsession with serial killers." The statement received no reaction from James, but set the tone of what was to come.

Mr. Spencer continued, "You have been immersed in that obsession for several months at least" and were "seeking to emulate others, such as Peter Sutcliffe, the Yorkshire Ripper." This was a reference by the trial judge of one incident where Peter Sutcliffe had purposely stabbed one of his victims in their eyes, which James had done to Nahid on purpose and James Attfield inadvertently at first. The courtroom was captivated by the judge's presentation. Anticipation built as the friends and families of the victims were hopeful James Fairweather would be sentenced to a long incarceration.

"I have no doubt the way James Attfield screamed in pain when he was stabbed through the eye had remained with you and excited you," Mr. Spencer added.

Mr. Spencer mentioned briefly that James was in therapy and, beyond his autism, the court psychologist felt James had "emerging psychopathic personality disorder." The people in the courtroom learned that James was responding well to treatment, but Mr. Spencer cautioned, "It is too early to say how your emerging psychopathic personality disorder will develop."

Had James been an adult when he killed Nahid and James, he could have been sentenced to an entire life sentence, especially because it was Mr. Spencer's opinion that James murdered two people with a "substantial degree of premeditation" with "sadistic" features. However, James was a juvenile, so the sentencing guidelines were different -- but they would have pretty much the same result.

James Fairweather was sentenced to be detained at "Her Majesty's pleasure." In essence, this was the same as a life sentence. James would serve a minimum of twenty-seven years minus 339 days for the days he was in custody on remand. There were a few small cheers and a moment of happiness inside the courtroom when the sentence was handed down.

"Thereafter, it will be for the Parole Board to decide when, if ever, you should be released. If you are ever released, you will remain on license for the rest of your life," Mr. Spencer finished. Some in the courtroom said the manner in which Mr. Spencer spoke to James was piercing, and it was clear the judge was disgusted by the teenaged serial killer in his courtroom.

As James was escorted away from the courtroom, he was seen mouthing to his parents, "I don't give a shit." This was not the first time James shrugged off his situation, and he appeared to have zero remorse for what he'd done. To date, James Fairweather has not made a statement about his case to anyone other than doctors and psychiatrists. There's no doubt in my mind James has no feelings and would kill again if set free.

James is housed at a secure psychiatric hospital where he continues treatment and his parents are hopeful he may someday be released. It remains to be seen if that will actually happen, but my gut tells me James Fairweather will never see light outside of custody ever again.

Chapter Seven: The Psychology of Serial Killer James Fairweather

We've already discussed at length autism and what, if anything, the disorder played in the case of James Fairweather. Most experts believe autism had nothing to do with why James Fairweather became a serial killer. Doctors and psychologists who've interviewed James have unanimously agreed that, along with autism, James also has "emerging psychopathic personality disorder."

Emerging psychopathic personality disorder is more commonly known as antisocial personality disorder, which until recently was known as psychopathy. As psychiatrists and mental health professionals explore and better understand humans, many more labels for what we do and how we behave are developed. Most experts would also agree that it's near impossible to keep up with all of the mental health issues people are experiencing across the globe. Based on what I've observed during my career, especially over the last seven years, I believe the number of people walking among us with mental health problems is steadily increasing.

With regard to James Fairweather, he clearly exhibited, and continues to display, many of the known symptoms or ideations of a person suffering from antisocial personality disorder. Interpersonal traits such as deceit, manipulation, lack of empathy, egocentricity, selfishness, lack of guilt or remorse, and shallow affect not only describe psychopathy but are also used to describe antisocial personality disorder. As we've seen, James Fairweather displayed, and continues to display, all of these traits. In the early 1980s, further terms were added to the disorder to include lying, truancy, stealing, and violations of social norms. Again, beside the truancy issue, James Fairweather exhibited these characteristics. The question is was James wired differently than other children or did something happen to unlock his socially unacceptable behavior?

We know at the age of six, James was quiet and somewhat reserved. Still, he hung out in social situations and was described as kind and charismatic. He played darts with his dad in social settings, and none of the early school reports for him suggested he was developing a personality disorder. This, then, suggests his socialization could be classified as normal.

At the age of twelve, more specifically after his grandmother passed away from cancer, James clearly changed, and for the worse. It was around this same time that fellow students took notice of his protruding ears and teased him daily about them. Some of the larger kids at school also bullied James. The combination of his grief for his grandmother passing and the embarrassment and rage he felt stemming from the bullying and teasing mushroomed inside his head causing him to erupt. In the beginning, he needed an outlet for his anger.

James began exploring violent video games, hardcore pornography, and began researching famous serial killers. He would spend hours each day watching violence, playing violent games, and reading about the terrible things serial killers had done to their victims. Somewhere along the line, his brain began to crave violence and he could not stop thinking about violence. This fascination with violence blurred his ability to clearly distinguish right from wrong. He became dependent on death and destruction and craved seeing it or "experiencing" it through online gaming. Nothing else mattered in his life more than death, mutilation, and destruction. There's no doubt his mind was completely warped by this time and it was only a matter of time before he would act out.

The next time someone tried to bully him at school, James head-butted one of the kids and pushed another one to the ground. He finally stood up for himself, and the feeling he had while doing so was euphoric, uplifting for a kid who had been beaten down socially by his peers. Seeing the child he head-butted bleeding and the other child rolling around on the ground crying made James feel good inside. For once in his life, he was in control, and he felt more powerful than he ever thought possible. Most kids who are being bullied who stand up for themselves eventually move on, and the kids who were bullying them find a new target. In the case of James Fairweather, he overly enjoyed hurting the two kids who had been bullying him, and he was not about to stop there. Everyone would pay for messing with him.

While leaving school one day, and after years of exposing himself to any piece of stimulation he could find about serial killers, murder, killing, death, and violence, James took another step toward fulfilling his fantasy of killing someone. He'd taken a fancy to knives a few months prior. He had several, some he stole or found, and he held them in his hands and stroked them on a daily basis. On this date, and while still in his school uniform, he entered a convenience store, grabbed a few items from the shelves and turned to leave. He was confronted by staff, and James, wearing a sick smile, produced a knife and threatened to kill everyone in the store. Once again, the power and control he had in that moment excited him to a point where he was turned on. James left the store feeling the best he had ever felt about his life that he could ever recall.

James would be apprehended after the robbery and brought to court. He had a pompous attitude toward the judge and did not express remorse. James felt liberated and it did not matter what the judge, his parents, the people at the store, or his school had to say about him. He was his own person and no one would tell him what to do ever again. James was placed on supervision for a year for the robbery and was supposed to remain inside his home unless he was going to school or escorted by his parents. That plan worked for the courts, but not for James.

While back at school, some of the students began bullying him again. This time, however, he did not react and kept a mental note of who was doing it. James was asked by a teacher what he wanted to be when he grew up, and he replied, "A murderer." Some students laughed at his reply, some were nervous. The teacher sent him to the office, but once again, nothing was done to curtail the menacing thoughts James had shared with students and teachers.

Recall that he also mentioned that he wanted to do a "Columbine-like" incident on campus. This statement made its way to teachers and school administration causing James to be sent home. After a few meetings, it was agreed James could come back to the school to finish his exams. However, he would be in a separate room, supervised by staff, and he would have to leave campus as soon as his exams were complete.

At the age of fifteen, three years after his grandmother had died, James finally decided to show everyone how powerful he'd become. Amidst the disgusting pornographic videos, the horror movies, books about killing, and his fascination with serial killers, James found time to hatch a plan to physically kill someone. He said voices told him to murder a person, and if he didn't, the voices would kill him. However, it seems the voices were a farce.

James was so obsessed with serial killers, especially Peter Sutcliffe, that he decided he wanted to be a serial killer. Unlike most serial killers, James did not have a specific target in mind. He would not know his later victims. He wanted to use a knife and he wanted to experience the rush of murdering a real person. James had "killed" thousands of people online in the gaming world, but it was time to feel what it would be like to kill a real person.

For two nights, he walked along the streets in Colchester looking for the right person to kill. He had a knife on him and he constantly played with it inside his coat pocket. On the third night, growing frustrated that he could not find a victim, he moved closer to more populated areas. He walked along Riverside Walk near the Riverside Pub and literally stumbled upon James Attfield. Mr. Attfield was passed out in the overgrowth. In a cowardly move, James Fairweather decided he would kill Mr. Attfield because he was asleep and he would have no chance to defend himself from James's attack. It was time for the bullied to become the bully. It was time to play out the sick and disgusting thoughts in his head -- thoughts fueled by hardcore porn, violent video games, and murderous horror movies.

Stabbing someone one hundred and two times, many of those stabs being in his victim's eyes, was an extreme overkill and certainly solidified the fact that James Fairweather had graduated from harrowing internal thoughts to taking action. His rage and insatiable quest to be a serial killer led to the death of James Attfield. He left the scene with no remorse and tried to dispose of evidence linking him to the horrific crime.

James then spent months searching for information about the murder -- about the total chaos he'd caused. He was as infatuated with what the police and locals were saying about the killing of James Attfield as he was with serial killing in general. At this point, James was a lost cause. Nothing and no one would have been able to right this ship.

Three months later, after growing bored with life and in the need of another fix by way of killing someone, James set out to find another potential victim. He walked along another Colchester trail and saw Nahid Almanea. He noticed there wasn't anyone around, making it a good time to strike. He also saw that the woman was wearing sunglasses. He recalled that one of Peter Sutcliffe's victims wore glasses and Peter stabbed his victim in the eyes. James became extremely excited because he felt he had an opportunity to kill again and he could emulate something a serial killer he idolized had once done.

In broad daylight with no regard for human life, James came up from behind and stabbed Nahid in her stomach causing her to bend over. He slapped her sunglasses off, knocked her to the ground, and jumped on top of her. He stabbed her repeatedly, including in her eyes. He killed her in another fit of rage and then left the scene with no remorse. In fact, he was on cloud nine and had a certain buzz about him, similar to what one experiences when ingesting narcotics. James also tried to dispose of the murder weapon. He returned home as though nothing had happened. Once the victim was discovered, he scoured the internet and media outlets hoping to read about the murder he committed.

As police stumbled and grasped at straws to find the killer of James Attfield and Nahid Almanea, James was interviewed for both murders. These interviews excited James, and he demonstrated superior manipulation skills while speaking to the police. Although his alibi was not verified, he remained out of custody and enjoyed toying with local law enforcement. Officially, James Fairweather was classified as a person of interest in both murders until being caught and charged with the murders.

James was not an idiot and understood his two killings had caused a great stir in the community. He decided to lie low for a bit, but after a while, the itch to feel immense power over another human before killing them prompted him to seek a third victim. This time, though, the would-be victim spotted him before it was too late. She called the police and they came to the area searching for a suspicious teenager.

As we've discussed, police found and apprehended James. He was wearing gloves and armed with a long knife. He spontaneously told the police he was searching for someone to kill ... and that he'd already killed two people. This single event blew the investigation into James Attfield's and Nahid Almanea's murders wide open. There is no doubt James would have killed the woman who called the police. Thankfully, her attention to detail and willingness to act saved her life and likely the lives of many other residents.

James Fairweather is one of the most disturbing people I've ever researched. I have not spoken to him. I've read his statements and watched him on video. It's my opinion that he desperately craved attention and deliberately killed people hoping to be just like Peter Sutcliffe. In his mind, he felt he could be a better serial killer than Peter Sutcliffe. I believe were he not apprehended he would not have stopped killing people. I believe somewhere along the line he would have launched an attack at his school and tried to kill his parents. The amount of excitement and joy he obtains from taking a human life should scare the hell out of anyone who is near him.

Chapter Eight: Conclusion

By definition and the behavior he's displayed, James Fairweather is clearly psychotic and a serial killer. Whatever label people want to place on him and his behavior after the fact does not matter to me. There is no doubt that if he is ever released from custody, he will kill again. He will continue to kill until he is apprehended or he himself is killed. In my opinion, no amount of therapy or testing or whatever radical new approach there might be will ever work on a person like James Fairweather. His enjoyment and the personal satisfaction he obtained while killing two people is too strong to defeat.

Violent video games, pornography, sensational horror movies, and books glorifying serial killers in the hands of a teenager in James's condition are a recipe for disaster. Millions of other children experience the same stimulus and do not become serial killers. Millions of other children are bullied and teased and do not become serial killers. So what, then, truly set James Fairweather off?

I believe he was close to his grandmother, perhaps closer to her than his own parents, and she would always be the one to comfort him when he'd had a bad day at school. Teenagers often talk about how their parents just don't understand them, but grandparents seem always to know when a scoop of ice cream or a gentle talk is needed to help a struggling teenager. When James's grandmother passed away, I think he probably lost the only person who he felt truly understood him. He lost his security blanket and it was likely a sad and frightening moment for him. I believe all of the emotions one feels when losing a loved one unlocked major psychological issues that had been repressed within James's mind. Everything he said and did after her funeral progressed to taking two human lives and he continues to show no remorse about what he's done.

I began this book discussing how I feel teenagers today are continually exposed to stimuli that are pointing them in the wrong direction. Children are preyed upon by billion-dollar video game and movie industries, and the only thing that sells anymore is violence. Teenagers are desensitized to death and destruction and, in my opinion, the media fuels this growing fire by reporting the vilest and most disgusting stories they can find. At some point, we owe it to our children, the future of our great planet, to get them into sports, band, clubs, volunteering, outside, or anything to keep their minds off of violence. Would removing all of the things James was infatuated with prevent him from being a serial killer? I don't think so. But leaving these things out there and "hoping kids turn out okay" is not a solution I'm prepared to hang my hat on. Not now, and not ever.

About the Author

Chris Swinney is a Police Officer in the San Francisco Bay area. His writing includes the bestselling '*Bill Dix Detective Series*' which are fiction books based on his experience as a cop.

Swinney has also written several bestselling true crime books:

- *Robert Pickton: The Pig Farmer Killer*
- *The Killer Handyman: The True Story of William Patrick Fyfe*
- *Robert Black: The True Story of a Child Rapist and Serial Killer from the UK*
- *Deadly Voices: The True Story of Serial Killer Herbert Mullin*
- *The Beast of Birkenshaw: The True Story of Serial Killer Peter Manuel*
- *The Clairemont Killer*

Chris is a big time supporter of Teachers, Parents, Law Enforcement, Doctors, Nurses, Firefighters, American Troops, Juvenile Diabetes Research, and children. He spends time volunteering for his church, at schools, he coaches, and every once in awhile he gets to go fly fishing.

Visit Chris's Publisher's Page:
http://rjpp.ca/CHRIS-SWINNEY

Amazon's Author Page:

http://amzn.to/1LukWVr

Acknowledgments and Sources

A very special thanks to Linda and Ken Thompson for tirelessly poring over my words and providing me great input.

Law Enforcement:

* Guilford Crown Court
* Essex Police
* Nick Alston, Police and Crime Commissioner, Essex Police
* Judge, Mr. Justice Robin Spencer, QC
* Old Bailey Court
* Prosecutor, Philip Bennetts, QC
* Assistant Chief Constable Steve Worron, Essex Police
* Detective Constable Jane Morgan, Essex Police

Acquaintances:

* Dr. Simon Hill (Fairweather's main doctor).
* Dr. Philip Joseph (Leading criminal psychiatrist).

Research:

* Essex Police reports.
* Court documents (where available).
* The Sun
* Snapper Media
* The Independent
* BBC News
* Daily Mirror
* Michelle Sadler (Believed to be the planned third victim).
* Julie Finch (James Attfield's mother).
* Daily Mail
* The Guardian
* Guernsey Press
* Daily Gazette
* Essex County Standard

* Yahoo.com

The Victims:

* James Attfield, age 33.

* Nahid Almanea, age 31.

65091669R00066

Made in the USA
San Bernardino, CA
27 December 2017